SITTING BULL

FAMOUS FIGURES OF THE AMERICAN FRONTIER

BILLY THE KID

BUFFALO BILL CODY

CRAZY HORSE

DAVY CROCKETT

GEORGE CUSTER

WYATT EARP

GERONIMO

JESSE JAMES

ANNIE OAKLEY

SITTING BULL

FAMOUS FIGURES OF

SITTING BULL

THE AMERICAN FRONTIER

HAL MARCOVITZ

CHELSEA HOUSE PUBLISHERS
PHILADELPHIA

Produced for Chelsea House by
OTTN Publishing, Stockton, NJ

CHELSEA HOUSE PUBLISHERS
Editor in Chief: Sally Cheney
Associate Editor in Chief: Kim Shinners
Production Manager: Pamela Loos
Art Director: Sara Davis
Series Designer: Keith Trego

First Printing

1 3 5 7 9 8 6 4 2

The Chelsea House World Wide Web address is
http://www.chelseahouse.com

Library of Congress Cataloging-in-Publication Data

Marcovitz, Hal.
Sitting Bull / by Hal Marcovitz.
    p.   cm. – (Famous figures of the American frontier)
Includes bibliographical references and index.
    ISBN 0-7910-6487-5 (alk. paper)
    ISBN 0-7910-6488-3 (pbk.: alk. paper)
1. Sitting Bull, 1834?-1890–Juvenile literature. 2. Dakota
Indians–Biography–Juvenile literature. 3. Hunkpapa
Indians–Biography–Juvenile literature. 4. Dakota Indians–
History–Juvenile literature. [1. Sitting Bull, 1834?-1890. 2.
Hunkpapa Indians–Biography. 3. Indians of North America–
Great Plains–Biography.] I. Title. II. Series.

E99.D1 S61235 2001
978.004'9752'0092–dc21
[B]   2001028849

CONTENTS

1 THE FOUR VIRTUES   7

2 THE SUN DANCE   13

3 THE TREATY OF PLENTY RATIONS   19

4 DEFENDING SIOUX LANDS   25

5 THE LITTLE BIGHORN   35

6 THE GHOST DANCE   49

CHRONOLOGY   58

GLOSSARY   60

FURTHER READING   62

INDEX   63

This sketch made by Sitting Bull shows the day he won his first glory in battle. The 14-year-old is riding down a Crow Indian. The image of a bull at the upper right is his signature. Four feathers are hanging from the shield pictured on Sitting Bull's horse. These represent what the Sioux considered the four virtues of manhood: bravery, fortitude, generosity, and wisdom.

THE FOUR VIRTUES

His father named him Jumping Badger. It was hardly a fitting name for a brave warrior of the Hunkpapa Sioux, but the boy was just a baby. His father, a Hunkpapa chief, promised to give his son a new name when he proved himself in battle.

As the boy grew older, he learned the ways of the Indians of the Great Plains. His uncle, Four Horns, paid particular attention to the boy's education, teaching him to ride a horse and handle the bow and *tomahawk*. These were the most important skills a boy of the Hunkpapa Sioux could learn. Soon he would be expected to join the men of the tribe on a hunt and, when necessary, in combat.

Over the years, there had been no new name from his father. Instead, because the boy rarely rushed into trouble or made unwise decisions, he was given the nickname Hunkesni, or in English, Slow. Although this was a name that paid respect to the boy's intelligence, it was hardly a name associated with bravery or skill as a hunter. Still, Slow was only 10 years old when he killed his first buffalo.

When Slow turned 14, he accompanied a war party of 10 Hunkpapa braves. The Hunkpapas were often at war with the Crow Indians. For years, Crow and Hunkpapa Indians had fought over hunting grounds along the Powder River in Montana. Now it appeared the two tribes would *skirmish* again. Slow's father had at first spoken out against the boy joining the war party, claiming he was too young to go to battle. However, Slow promised to stay out of the actual fighting, and his father gave in and let him come along.

The war party searched for the Crows for three days. Finally, they spotted a dozen Crow warriors camped by a creek at the bottom of a slope. Whooping and shouting, the Hunkpapa warriors raced down the slope. The Crow warriors were startled by the surprise attack, but one Crow managed to mount his horse and escape. Slow, who was riding a swift gray horse his father had given him, decided to chase the escaping Crow.

Slow soon overtook the Crow and, using his tomahawk, struck the man and knocked him off his horse. Another Hunkpapa quickly caught up and finished off the wounded Crow.

"When fourteen years of age I went on my first warpath against a neighboring tribe. I distinguished myself for my bravery," Slow later said.

Back at the Crows' camp along the creek, the attack had been a success. Eight of the Crows had been killed by the attacking Sioux Indians. The other four managed to escape, and they would no doubt spread the story of how the young boy had led the fierce Hunkpapa attack against their people.

As for Slow, he was given a hero's welcome when the war party returned to the Hunkpapa village. His father gave a magnificent feast to honor his

Seth Eastman painted this Sioux dwelling in Minnesota around 1847. Slow, the Hunkpapa Sioux who would become known as Sitting Bull, probably lived in a house such as this when he was growing up in the 1830s and 1840s.

son. He presented the boy with a white eagle's feather to be worn in his hair as a symbol of bravery. He gave his son a new horse, even faster than the gray horse Slow had ridden in the attack on the Crow.

Next, he gave Slow a *lance* and a shield. The lance was carved from an ash tree and decorated with blue and white beads. A notched iron blade was fastened to the tip. The lance was more than seven feet long and would serve the boy well in battles to come. The shield was crafted from tough buffalo hide, and Slow's father told the boy it would endow him with sacred powers. The design on Slow's shield was a bold figure of a bird painted in red, green, blue, and brown. Four eagle feathers hung from the shield's frame, signifying the four virtues of Hunkpapa manhood: bravery, *fortitude*, generosity, and wisdom. As a man, Slow would be expected to live up to those virtues.

Finally, the boy's father gave him a new name. No longer would he be known as Jumping Badger or the nickname Slow. Instead, the father named the boy Tatanka-Iyotanka. In English, those words mean Sitting Bull—an animal of great endurance and strength, immovable and ready to fight to the death.

This Sioux picture-writing, done on the hide of a bison, depicts the Sun Dance. This religious ceremony was done to thank the sun for past favors, and to request renewed protection for the tribe. The cross at the center of the circle represents the presence of a white man at the ceremony.

THE SUN DANCE

Sitting Bull was born in March 1831 in what is now South Dakota. Sitting Bull's mother was named Her Holy Door. His father was also called Sitting Bull. However, after giving this name to his 14-year-old son following the attack on the Crows, he changed his own name to Jumping Bull. Over the years, Sitting Bull would travel with his people throughout South Dakota, particularly in an area in the western part of the state known as the Black Hills. His people also made their homes in North Dakota and Montana. In fact, Sioux Indians are also called Dakota Indians. In some Sioux dialects, the name is pronounced Lakota.

The name Dakota comes from the Sioux word for "friends." The Hunkpapas were one tribe of the Sioux nation, which was composed of seven tribes spread throughout the West. The others were the Oglala, Brulé, Miniconjou, Two Kettle, Sans Arc, and Sihasapa Sioux.

During Sitting Bull's boyhood, few white settlers traveled to Montana and the Dakotas. The Oregon Trail, which led settlers to the Pacific Coast, cut through Nebraska and Wyoming, well to the south of Hunkpapa Sioux territory. Mostly, the white men the Sioux encountered were trappers. These men were more interested in making friends and trading with the Sioux than in pushing the Indians off their land.

As a young boy, Sitting Bull learned how to make his own weapons, particularly the bow. He carved his bows from orange Osage wood. Each had to be five feet or more in length. He also

This painting of a buffalo hunt on the Southwestern prairies was made in 1845. The buffalo was essential to the Sioux way of life. The tribe ate the meat of the enormous animals, made clothes and dwellings from their skins, and used their bones and sinews to fashion tools and utensils.

learned how to hunt buffalo. The meat from the enormous animals provided food for the tribe, and the tough buffalo hides could be fashioned into clothes, shoes, and fabric to cover tepees.

To hunt buffalo, the warriors would assemble on the prairie, always facing west in a crescent *formation*. A painted stone that would serve as an altar was placed at the center of the crescent. One of the hunters would smoke a ceremonial pipe. Then he would raise the stone above his head and swear a tribute to Wakan Tanka, the great spirit of the Sioux people, and Tatanka, the buffalo god. Each hunter would then take his turn smoking the pipe.

The ceremony now over, the hunters would mount their horses and fan out in search of a buffalo herd. They would use their sturdy Osage bows to slay the animals.

Sitting Bull and his young friends were free to explore the Dakota wilderness, eat when they were hungry, and sleep when they became tired. Adults never struck children, but they wanted to make sure their boys grew up tough and ready to fight. *Valor* was highly regarded among Sioux warriors. So they encouraged their sons to play games and undergo rituals that posed some degree of physical danger; they wanted the boys to learn to experience physical pain.

When Sitting Bull was a young man, he participated in his first *Sun Dance*. In this ritual, Sioux men renewed their friendships, danced, feasted, and shared stories.

To participate in the Sun Dance, Sitting Bull and the other young Sioux men first had to undergo purification in a sweat bath. They had to strip off their clothes and sit in a tepee filled with steam from water boiled over hot stones. After enduring the hot temperatures, the young warriors left the tepee to perform a ceremonial dance around the Sun Dance pole. Finally, a tribe member approached each warrior and cut four-inch slits in his chest and back. Pointed sticks tied to rawhide thongs were inserted into the slits, and the thongs were then tossed over the crossbar of the Sun Dance pole. The warriors were hoisted off their feet and left to dangle in excruciating pain until they could wriggle free on their own.

It took Sitting Bull some 30 minutes to free himself from the Sun Dance pole. Finally, free of the painful sticks, he was forced to dance for the next day and night until he collapsed in exhaustion. Only by participating in this Sun Dance ritual could a Hunkpapa Sioux warrior prove that he was truly fearless and immune to pain.

The Treaty of
Plenty
Rations

Sitting Bull grew into a brawny and muscular warrior. He stood 5 feet 10 inches tall. He had a broad nose and sharp features that appeared to have been carved from stone. In Sioux custom, he wore his shiny black hair long and parted in the middle.

By the 1850s, settlers were making their way west in wagon trains along the Oregon Trail. The United States government intended to protect them from Native American attacks. In 1851, the government invited many Indian chiefs to Fort Laramie in Wyoming and asked them to sign a treaty that would ensure the safety of the settlers. The treaty promised food, clothing, blankets, and other *provisions* for the Indians in exchange for their promise not to harass settlers on the Oregon Trail. As part of the treaty, the chiefs were also asked to permit the government to build military outposts on their land. Finally, the treaty promised to protect the Indians against the white man's aggression. The chiefs called the pact the "Treaty of Plenty Rations."

The Oregon Trail was south of Hunkpapa land. Nevertheless, the Hunkpapas sent representatives to the council. Hunkpapa chiefs touched the pen used by the white officials to sign the chiefs' names. That meant they had approved the treaty.

It didn't take long for both sides to break the treaty. The Native Americans quickly found that they were receiving less food than they had expected. Meanwhile, the Indians of Wyoming–the Oglala and Brulé Sioux–found that the noisy and dust-stirring wagon trains were driving the game away. Angry Sioux warriors responded by harassing the wagon trains. That brought a swift and violent response from the *cavalry* troops stationed in the forts the Sioux had permitted on their land.

On August 19, 1854, the pot was stirred to a boil when a young army lieutenant named John L.

Grattan led 30 soldiers into a Brulé village near Fort Laramie. He demanded that the tribe turn over an Indian who had killed an ox that had strayed from a wagon train. When Chief Conquering Bear refused, Grattan ordered his men to open fire. Conquering Bear fell dead, but the warriors in his tribe retaliated, killing Grattan and all his men.

The U.S. Army's *reprisal* was brutal. In the spring of 1855, troops led by General William S. Harney went on a swift and bloody march. As the soldiers made their way north into Hunkpapa territory, they attacked villages and murdered warriors, women, and children. The march ended in October 1855 at Fort Pierre. The Indians were so terrified of Harney that they named him "Mad Bear." They called the soldiers "Long Knives" because of the *bayonets* they carried on their rifles.

On March 1, 1856, Harney summoned the Sioux chiefs to a council at Fort Pierre to draw up a treaty. Four Horns attended the council, as did Sitting Bull, who was still a young warrior.

Harney told the Sioux that if they continued to attack wagon trains, they would be punished by the U.S. Army. Even worse, the general insisted that he would appoint the tribal chiefs. Four Horns bristled at this insult. Who was this white man to tell Hunkpapas that he had the authority to name their chief? But Harney would not back down. He named Bear's Rib chief of the Hunkpapa Sioux, and rode off, leaving Bear's Rib in command of the supplies that were to be distributed under the Treaty of Plenty Rations.

> Many of the Hunkpapas believed Bear's Rib lacked the courage of a true warrior. He had always advocated negotiations rather than war with the white men. Young Sioux warriors were taught to endure great physical pain and prove their valor on the battlefield, not to agree to terms dictated by an outsider.

By the early 1860s, white settlers were pushing their way further north, intruding on the Hunkpapa hunting grounds in the Dakotas and Montana. The wagon trains scattered buffalo herds and trampled over prairie grass that the Sioux depended on to feed their horses. And in 1862, gold was discovered in Montana. That year, more than 500 *prospectors* rode steamboats up the Missouri River to Fort Benton in Montana. With gold miners trampling on their hunting grounds, the Hunkpapas were unable to live under Mad Bear Harney's treaty. They started attacking the steamboats while they sailed up the Missouri. In nearby Minnesota, hundreds of settlers died in an Indian attack.

Finally, by the summer of 1863 the attacks had become so numerous that the army had to act. The Union Army diverted a division of troops from the Civil War in the South and sent it into the Dakotas to keep the peace. Now it was official: the U.S. Army was at war with the Hunkpapa Sioux. It was a war that would not end for nearly 30 years.

The Long Knives clearly had the upper hand. In July 1863, Sioux warriors were defeated by the soldiers at the battles of Dead Buffalo Lake and Stony Lake. It is likely that Sitting Bull fought in both battles. The Indians would suffer more defeats as the year dragged on.

By 1865, Sitting Bull had proven himself in battle many times. He was approached by tribal leaders and asked to take over the Hunkpapa tribe. Bear's Rib had been murdered by Hunkpapa warriors who could not tolerate his willingness to live at peace with the whites. Sitting Bull, who was among the most militant in his views against white settlement in Hunkpapa country, quickly agreed to the wishes of the tribal elders.

He was now chief of the Hunkpapa Sioux.

DEFENDING SIOUX LANDS

4

A herd of buffalo graze in the foothills of South Dakota's Black Hills. This area was the center of the Sioux world. To Sitting Bull and his people, the Black Hills were holy mountains where warriors could speak with Wakan Tanka, the Great Spirit.

By 1866, the army had built Fort Reno, Fort Phil Kearny, and Fort C. F. Smith along a new trail that cut through Wyoming and Montana. It was known as the Bozeman Trail, and it led prospectors to the gold fields in Montana. In North Dakota, the army built Fort Buford at the *confluence* of the Missouri and Yellowstone Rivers. This fort was in the heart of

This marker shows where the Bozeman Trail began, near Fort Fetterman, Wyoming. The fort was named for a U.S. Army officer who was killed, along with 80 of his men, in an ambush by the Oglala Sioux warrior Crazy Horse.

Hunkpapa hunting grounds.

Sitting Bull led an attack on Fort Buford on December 22, 1866. His warriors captured the fort's ice house and sawmill and set fire to the fort's winter supply of firewood. But they were eventually driven off by cannon fire from the walled stockade. The Hunkpapas returned repeatedly during the winter to harass the Long Knives in the fort.

Meanwhile, more forts were going up along the Missouri River. Now that the Civil War was over, the army had plenty of troops to send to Montana and the Dakotas to fight Native Americans. By 1868, the army had ringed all of Sioux land with military outposts. The Sioux were surrounded, but Sitting Bull resolved to fight on.

"I have killed, robbed and injured too many whites," he said. "They are medicine and I would eventually die a lingering death. I had rather die on the field of battle."

Father Pierre-Jean De Smet, a Catholic priest, entered Sioux territory in the spring of 1868. He was called Black Robe by the Indians. Sitting Bull was told the priest was traveling with a message of peace, carrying a new treaty written by the Indian Department in Washington. De Smet hoped to convince the Sioux chiefs to end the bloodshed and agree to its terms.

Father De Smet met Sitting Bull and the leaders of the other Sioux tribes on June 20, 1868, on the Yellowstone River near the Powder River in Montana. He arrived just as the tribes were preparing for the ritual of the Sun Dance.

The chiefs gathered in a huge council lodge, made up of ten tepees. Representing the Hunkpapas were Sitting Bull; his uncle Four Horns; Black Moon, the Hunkpapa spiritual leader; and three war chiefs: Gall, White Gut, and No Neck.

The Sioux chiefs opened the council by performing a ceremonial dance and sharing a peace

SITTING BULL'S FAMILY LIFE

Family life was very important to Sioux men. After a day of hunting or battle, they wanted to come home and enjoy the company of wives and children. So in 1851, at the age of 20, Sitting Bull married Tatiyopa, a young woman from his village. She died giving birth to his first son, who died of disease at the age of four. Sitting Bull was grief-stricken at the loss of his son. To ease his troubled heart, he adopted his nephew One Bull and raised him as his own son.

He would marry again. Sioux custom permitted warriors to take multiple wives. Sitting Bull soon married Snow-on-Her, with whom he had two daughters, and Red Woman, who delivered a son to her new husband. He often quarreled with Snow-on-Her. He eventually divorced her in a ceremony in which he beat on a drum and announced the marriage over. Sitting Bull insisted on raising the two daughters, and they remained in his tepee.

Some years later, Red Woman also fell ill and died. Now he had pipe with De Smet and his interpreters. It was then up to the priest to lay out the government's terms. He told the chiefs that the army would abandon three forts along the Bozeman Trail. Some 20 million acres of land would be set aside for a Great

lost two wives through disease and a third through divorce. Responsible for raising his three surviving children, Sitting Bull asked for help from his sister Good Feather. She moved into his tepee to look after the children.

When he reached his thirties, Sitting Bull took two more wives: Four Robes and her widowed sister, Seen-by-the-Nation, who

Sitting Bull and members of his family outside his tepee, in a photo taken in the late 1880s.

already had two sons. The two women and two young boys moved into Sitting Bull's tepee. There was room. Indeed, Sitting Bull's tepee was the largest in the village. It measured 12 feet in diameter and required four buffalo robes to cover the floor.

Pierre Jean De Smet was a Jesuit missionary who had worked among the Indians of the west for decades. He visited Sitting Bull's camp in 1868 and tried to convince the Sioux leader to sign the Fort Laramie Treaty.

Sioux *Reservation*–the land would be west of the Missouri River in North Dakota and South Dakota. No whites would be allowed to "pass over, settle upon or reside on" the reservation without permission of the Sioux. In return, the Plains Indians would surrender all the rest of their land to the government, although they would be permitted to hunt buffalo in territory that spanned west from the Dakotas to the Bighorn Mountains in Wyoming.

"This cruel and unfortunate war must be stopped, not only on account of your children, but for a thousand other reasons," the priest told the chiefs. "Forget the past, and accept the offering of peace which is now just sent you."

Sitting Bull turned to De Smet and gave him his response. It was quick and decisive: "I wish all to know I do not propose to sell any part of my country . . . those forts filled with white soldiers must be abandoned; there is no greater source of trouble and grievance to my people."

The council was over. The war would go on.

All but the Brulé Sioux refused to sign the treaty. Four Horns now realized that the war would get even bloodier. He knew that the Sioux had to unite themselves as they had never been united before. That meant the seven tribes would need one strong leader. So he sent *emissaries* to the other Sioux tribes, proposing that a supreme chief of the Sioux be named. He wanted his nephew Sitting Bull elected supreme chief.

In 1869, six Sioux tribal chiefs met at a council in a forest they called Rainy Buttes along the Cannonball River in North Dakota. Only the Brulé Sioux were not represented; they had moved onto the reservation. The chiefs at the council agreed to make Sitting Bull head of what they called the Sioux Nation. "Because of your bravery on the battlefield, as the bravest warrior in all our bands, we have elected you head chief of the entire Sioux nation, head war chief," Four Horns told his nephew. "When you tell us to fight, we shall fight. When you say make peace, we shall make peace."

Sitting Bull had no intention of making peace.

⚜⚜⚜⚜

By the early 1870s, the Hunkpapas found themselves fighting the Crows as much as the Long Knives. Buffalo were growing scarce in the Hunkpapa hunting grounds, and the Sioux were becoming desperate for the animals.

There was virtually no part of the buffalo that the Native Americans did not use. Buffalo meat provided the Indians with food. Buffalo hides could be used to make the covers and floors for their tepees, as well as clothes, shoes, and blankets. The bones of the buffalo could be carved into tools, eating utensils, and weapons. Buffalo fat was boiled into glue.

In the Sioux language, Hunkpapa means "People who camp at the entrance." To Sioux Indians, it meant they were people who defended their land to the death.

But the buffalo herds had roamed west into Crow land, and the Hunkpapas were forced to follow them and fight the Crows for the right to hunt the beasts. The Crows and Hunkpapas skirmished often, attacking each other's hunting parties.

While the tribes were fighting, they hardly noticed new white activity in their lands. In the fall of 1871, *surveyors* escorted by 600 soldiers appeared in the Yellowstone Valley in Montana to survey for a railroad. They were planning a route for the Northern Pacific Railroad, which would link St. Paul, Minnesota, with Seattle, Washington.

Sitting Bull sent Black Moon, the Hunkpapa spiritual leader, to tell the surveyors they were intruding on Sioux land. The surveyors, with the soldiers behind them, refused to leave. Surveying parties would return many times over the next two years, and they would always be escorted by many soldiers. With the war against the Crow Indians occupying the Sioux warriors, Sitting Bull could do little to drive the railroad men off Hunkpapa land. Finally, in the summer of 1873, the surveyors arrived in the sacred Indian land of the Black Hills in South Dakota.

They were accompanied by the U.S. Army's Seventh Cavalry, which was under the command of an officer with shoulder-length, red-gold hair. His name was George Armstrong Custer.

THE LITTLE
BIGHORN

This painting, *Call of the Bugle*, shows the final defeat of Custer and his men on Last Stand Hill. Sitting Bull was among the Sioux warriors who defeated the Seventh Cavalry in the June 1876 battle.

The Sioux called the Black Hills "Paha Sapa," which means "Hills that are Black." The dark, towering hills rise some 4,000 feet into the sky, providing a stark contrast to the yellow prairies that surround them. The Black Hills had tremendous spiritual significance to the Sioux. They believed this region in western South Dakota to be the most sacred of their lands. Even the

Indian Department in Washington recognized their importance to the Sioux. In 1868, the Black Hills were included in Father De Smet's treaty, promised to the Sioux as part of the Great Sioux Reservation.

"We want no white men here," Sitting Bull would say later. "The Black Hills belong to me. If the whites try to take them, I will fight."

Unknown to Sitting Bull, though, rumors had spread among the whites that the Black Hills were rich in gold. Those rumors spread quickly, and gold miners flocked to Paha Sapa. They did not care about the terms of Father De Smet's treaty, not when gold was in the hills.

Now the Sioux saw many intruders in their most sacred land. And protecting them were soldiers of the U.S. Army, led by Custer, whom the Indians nicknamed "Long Hair."

⁂

The story of Lieutenant Colonel George Armstrong Custer and the battle of the Little Bighorn River is truly an American legend. Certainly, it has been recorded in military history as one of the U.S. Army's most catastrophic blunders. Yet Custer is mostly remembered as a valiant and dashing American hero.

He was born in 1839 in Ohio and educated at the U.S. Military Academy at West Point, N.Y. By the time he graduated from West Point, the nation was *immersed* in the Civil War. Custer became a cavalry officer and rose quickly in the ranks. Within two years of his graduation at West Point, he was promoted to brigadier general. At age 23, he was the youngest general in the U.S. Army. He saw action in many of the great Civil War battles, including Gettysburg, where cavalry troops under his command defeated a fierce regiment of rebel horsemen under the leadership of General J. E. B. Stuart.

After the war, Custer's rank was lowered to lieutenant colonel and he was sent west to fight Indians. By the 1870s, his job mostly required him to ensure the safety of the railroad men. Custer regarded this job as vital if the country intended to fulfill its Manifest Destiny. "The experience of the past, particularly of recent years, has shown that no one measure so quickly and effectually frees a country from the horrors and devastations of Indian wars and Indian depredations generally as the building and successful operation of a railroad," he wrote in March 1873, while leading the Seventh Cavalry through the Dakotas.

This painting of George A. Custer hangs in the U.S. Military Academy at West Point. During the Civil War, Custer became the youngest general in the U.S. Army. After the war, Custer was demoted in rank to lieutenant colonel and sent west to fight Indians on the frontier.

By 1874, Custer was leading a peacekeeping force of cavalry soldiers through the Black Hills. The Indians had a name for the dusty trail Custer and his supply wagons had cut through Paha Sapa. They called it the "Thieves' Road."

In September 1875, Sitting Bull and other chiefs were summoned to a council with white officials from Washington. The white men wished to make a new treaty offer to the Indians. At first, Sitting Bull refused to go to the council. He remembered the Treaty of Plenty Rations, which had failed to provide the abundant food and clothing that had been promised the Sioux in 1851. He also remembered the humiliation Mad Bear Harney had made the Sioux suffer when he told them he would appoint their chiefs. And he remembered Father De Smet's treaty of 1868, which would have forced them to live on the Great Sioux Reservation. So he selected an emissary to send to the council.

"I want you to go and tell the Great Father that I do not want to sell any land to the government," Sitting Bull said. And then he stooped down and picked up a pinch of dirt, holding it between two fingers. He said, "Not even as much as this."

Soon, though, Sitting Bull had a change of heart, so he traveled to the White River in South Dakota to hear the white man's offer. The government offered money and supplies. In exchange, white prospectors would be allowed to search for gold in the Black Hills.

The Indians refused. The idea of giving white men permission to dig up the sacred lands of Paha Sapa was inconceivable. The government officials returned to Washington with no signed treaty. Instead, they issued warnings to the War Department that bloody Indian attacks on miners and railroad crews were more likely now than ever.

The official request to buy mining rights in the Black Hills was made by U.S. Senator William B. Allison of Iowa, who asked:

> We now have to ask you if you are willing to give our people the right to mine in the Black Hills as long as gold or other valuable minerals are found, for a fair and just sum. If you are so willing, we will make a bargain with you for this right. When the gold or other valuable materials are taken away, the country will again be yours to dispose of in any manner you may wish.

When Allison was turned down by Sitting Bull and the other Sioux leaders, he returned to Washington and issued warnings to the War Department that bloody Indian attacks on miners and railroad crews were more likely now than ever. Allison recommended to Congress that the government send in the military and take the lands from the Sioux.

So they recommended to Congress that the government go ahead with plans to seize the lands from the Native Americans by force.

The next move came when Edward P. Smith, commissioner of Indian Affairs, ordered the Sioux to settle on the Great Reservation by January 31, 1876. Otherwise, "military force would be sent to compel them." Again, the Sioux refused.

On March 17, 1876, the Long Knives attacked. A

column of soldiers led by Colonel Joseph J. Reynolds swept through a camp of Oglala Sioux near the Powder River in Montana. The Long Knives destroyed the village and killed many women and children.

Fearing more attacks, the Oglalas and their chief, Crazy Horse, made their way west to the Tongue River, where Sitting Bull and the Hunkpapas were camped. Also joining them were many Cheyenne Indians.

It has long been debated by historians how many Native Americans were now concentrated in this area of southern Montana, between the Tongue and Little Bighorn Rivers. Later in the year, following the battle of the Little Bighorn, the U.S. Army issued a report stating that the Sioux alone numbered 25,000 members. This included a fighting force of some 12,000 warriors.

But prior to the battle, the army had a much different assessment of the strength of Sitting Bull's warriors. A *Chicago Tribune* reporter traveling with the army wrote, "For nearly two weeks, this command has been marching through the best part of the whole unceded Sioux lands, and it has not seen 1,000 Indians in all. I doubt if there are 3,000 hostile people south of the Missouri and east of the Big Horn Mountains."

Most likely, the number of warriors Custer encountered at the Little Bighorn River numbered somewhere between the army's post-battle estimate of 12,000 and the newspaper reporter's count of 3,000. One fact remains clear: the number of men under Long Hair Custer's command at the battle of Little Bighorn numbered a mere 650.

ʑ▲ʑ▲ʑ▲ʑ▲

The Long Knives planned an attack on the Sioux and Cheyenne that they believed would once and for all end the Indian wars. Leading one force against the Sioux would be General George Crook. A second force would be led by Long Hair Custer.

The first skirmish occurred on the night of June 17, 1876. Crazy Horse's warriors attacked Crook's men near a Sioux village on the nearby Rosebud River. Most of the battle was fought under the cover of darkness. As dawn broke, Crazy Horse saw a column of Crook's troops leaving the battlefield in retreat. The Sioux had beaten the Long Knives at what would be called the Battle of the Rosebud.

After the battle, Crazy Horse and the other chiefs decided to move their camps to the Little Bighorn

This pictograph (picture writing) was made by an Oglala Sioux named Amos Bad Heart Bull. It shows Sitting Bull and Crazy Horse addressing a group of Sioux warriors before the Battle of the Little Bighorn. When Crazy Horse and the Oglalas arrived at Sitting Bull's camp, they found the Hunkpapa Sioux chief preparing for a Sun Dance. Sitting Bull went through the bloody ritual, then danced by the Sun Dance pole for three days. After the ceremony, he told the tribal leaders that he had a vision. He had seen Long Knives falling like grasshoppers from the sky.

River. They thought the buffalo hunting would be better there.

Six Sioux tribes as well as the Cheyennes made camp along the Little Bighorn. On the morning of June 25, scouting parties observed Custer leading a group of about 264 Seventh Cavalry soldiers west toward the Little Bighorn. One Sioux woman who saw the column advance toward the river was Sitting Bull's cousin, Pretty White Cow. Later, she said, "We could see the flashing of their sabres and saw that there were very many soldiers in the party."

Meanwhile, a second Seventh Cavalry column led by Major Marcus Reno also approached the Sioux camp from the south. Gall, a Hunkpapa chief whom Sitting Bull regarded as a brother, led the attack on Reno's men. At first, Reno's troops fired into the village, killing women and children. All of Gall's family was wiped out in the attack. "It made my heart bad," Gall told a newspaper reporter years later. "After that I killed all my enemies with the hatchet."

Gall's men quickly ***retaliated*** and drove Reno's troops into the woods. The soldiers were soon routed, but the major as well as most of his men managed to escape. Of the 150 men under his command, 18 were killed and 46 wounded.

Custer's troops would not be so lucky. Gall's men met them, as did warriors under Crazy Horse and a force of Cheyenne Indians. They trapped the Seventh Calvary on a hill overlooking the Little Bighorn. Soon, they surrounded the greatly out-numbered Long Knives.

This 19th-century illustration shows Custer carrying a saber and blazing away at the attacking Sioux and Cheyenne warriors with two pistols. Actually, Custer and his men left their sabers behind at the fort; they were armed with Springfield rifles and Colt pistols. Also, the Seventh Cavalry leader cut his hair short before the campaign, and fought Sitting Bull's forces in a flannel shirt and a buckskin jacket and pants.

Pretty White Cow described what happened next: "The smoke of the shooting and the dust of the horses shut out the hill. The soldiers fired many shots, but the Sioux shot straight and the soldiers fell dead. The women crossed the river after the men of

This Native American picture-writing shows Sioux and Cheyenne warriors leaving the battlefield after their victory over Custer and the Seventh Cavalry.

our village, and when we came to the hill there were no soldiers living and Long Hair lay dead among the rest. The blood of the people was hot and their hearts bad, and they took no prisoners that day."

After the battle, several warriors took credit for killing Custer. Many of the warriors admitted, though, that they had not recognized Long Hair during the battle.

Sitting Bull, who had witnessed the battle,

claimed to have watched Custer die.

"He did not wear his long hair as he used to wear it," said Sitting Bull. "It was short, and it was the color of the grass when the frost comes. Where the last stand was made, the Long Hair stood like a sheaf of corn with all the ears fallen around him."

This portrait of Sitting Bull was painted in 1899 by Catherine Weldon, a wealthy woman from New York who was sympathetic to the chief's cause. When Sitting Bull was arrested and killed a year later, one of the arresting officers slashed the portrait as well.

THE GHOST DANCE

The story of the Seventh Cavalry's defeat traveled quickly across the country. Americans were appalled at what they regarded as the savage slaughter of soldiers. It was a time of intense patriotism in the United States. Just nine days after the battle of the Little Bighorn, the nation would celebrate its *centennial* on July 4, 1876. Few people regarded the Indians' attack on Custer's men as a justified defense of their village and the sacred grounds of the Black Hills.

In Washington, Congress granted more money to the army and gave it the *mandate* to put down the Indian uprising. Congress also declared the Treaty of Plenty Rations broken by the Sioux and ceased food shipments to the Native Americans living on the Great Reservation. But the lawmakers in Washington offered a new treaty: food in exchange for the Black Hills. Faced with the starvation of their people, the Sioux chiefs were forced to sign over their lands.

Meanwhile, the army intended to carry out its mandate to wipe out the Indian threat. Thousands of soldiers flooded into the Dakotas and Montana. The Indians unlucky enough to be caught in the crossfire were brutally slaughtered.

On September 9, 1876, a battalion dispatched by General Crook swept through a village of Miniconjou Sioux families camped at the Slim Buttes near the Killdeer Mountains in North Dakota. On November 25, Crook struck again, burning two Cheyenne villages in the Bighorn Mountains in Wyoming. A total of 40 men, women, and children were killed.

Sitting Bull and the Hunkpapas found themselves skirmishing with troops under the command of Colonel Nelson Miles. The Indians called him Bear Coat Miles because he wore a fur-trimmed coat. With Miles harassing Hunkpapa villages, Sitting Bull decided to lead his people to Canada. There they would be free from the constant fear of the U.S. Army. In May 1877, a thousand Hunkpapa Sioux followed their chief to a camp in the Wood Mountains, about 40 miles north of the Montana border in Saskatchewan.

For now, they were safe. The Indians found plenty of buffalo to hunt and Canadians willing to trade with them. After about a year, the Hunkpapas were joined by about 800 members of the Nez Percé tribe who had also been driven off their land by the Long Knives. The camp further swelled when Oglalas fleeing the Long Knives crossed the border. By the spring of 1878, some 5,000 Native Americans were camped in Canada's Wood Mountains.

Such a concentration of Indians was alarming to the Canadian government. It did not want to deal with the same problem of what to do with the Indians that had plagued the United States government for years. By 1880, buffalo in the Wood

Mountains were growing scarce. The Indians were forced to cross the Montana border to hunt. These hunting trips often caught the attention of the Long Knives, who would chase the hunters back into Canada. In May 1880, Sitting Bull sent an emissary to Fort Buford on the Missouri River in North Dakota. He asked what would happen to the Sioux if they chose to return. He was told the Indians would be expected to surrender unconditionally, give up their weapons, and live on the Great Sioux Reservation.

His people hungry and nearly naked, Sitting Bull decided the Hunkpapas could no longer hold out. On July 12, 1881, Sitting Bull led the Hunkpapas back across the Montana border. Seven days later, they arrived at Fort Buford and surrendered.

The Sioux settled on part of the Great Sioux Reservation near Standing Rock, along the Missouri River in North and South Dakota.

As his fame as the "killer of Custer" grew, Sitting Bull became something of a celebrity. He marched in a parade with former President Ulysses S. Grant and was asked to visit schools, government offices, and factories to talk about his experiences. As the years went by, he was forgiven for the Little

Bighorn. More and more people realized that Custer had made a mistake by foolishly leading a small column of men against an overwhelming enemy force.

In 1885, Sitting Bull joined Buffalo Bill Cody's Wild West Show. The show toured cities across the country, featuring a variety of cowboy acts, such as fancy rope tricks, sharpshooting, and acrobatic horseback riding. Buffalo Bill Cody was a colorful cowboy hero who had ridden for the Pony Express, an early mail delivery route through the western territories. For $50 a week, Sitting Bull rode in the opening parade, appeared briefly in the arena, and greeted visitors in his tepee, where he sold photographs of himself.

> When Sitting Bull surrendered, he gave his rifle to his young son, Crow Foot. He instructed the boy to present the rifle to Major David H. Brotherton, commander of Fort Buford. Sitting Bull said: "I surrender this rifle to you through my young son, whom I now desire to teach in this manner that he has become a friend of the Americans. I wish him to learn the habits of the whites and to be educated as their sons are educated. I wish it to be remembered that I was the last man of my tribe to surrender my rifle."

Buffalo Bill and Sitting Bull pose together in this photo taken in Montreal, Canada, in 1885. For a short time Sitting Bull was one of the main attractions of the Wild West Show.

Sitting Bull remained with the Wild West Show for four months, but grew uncomfortable living among the white men. "I would rather die an Indian than live a white man," he said. He returned to Standing Rock, where one final battle awaited him.

In 1888, the government in Washington needed land for the thousands of **homesteaders** who had been moving west. The government decided to take it from the Sioux. Of the 20 million acres of the Great Sioux Reservation, 9 million were to be turned over to white homesteaders. At first the government offered to compensate the Sioux by paying 50 cents an acre. Sitting Bull convinced the other chiefs not to sign the agreement. However, all but Sitting Bull ultimately caved in to the government's pressure to sell the reservation land. "There are no Indians left but me," Sitting Bull said bitterly.

While leaders in Washington planned this latest scheme to steal Sioux land, an Indian in Nevada named Wovoka had started a new religion, the "Ghost Dance." Ghost dancers wore shirts painted with the sun, moon, stars, and planets; they danced until they fell from exhaustion, at which time others took their places.

> Sitting Bull had once had a vision in which an eagle told him that he would lead the Sioux people. In 1889, he had another vision. "The Sioux will kill you," he was informed by a meadowlark.

At the conclusion of the dance, Wovoka preached, the old ways would return. White men would leave Indian lands, buffalo would return, and Indians would be free to hunt and live as they did before the settlers, miners, and railroad men stole their land.

News of the Ghost Dance spread throughout the reservations. Soon, Hunkpapas at Standing Rock practiced the Ghost Dance. In Washington, officials believed that the Ghost Dance would prompt the Hunkpapas to become hostile again. They were concerned that Sitting Bull, their great war chief, still lived among them. So they ordered Sitting Bull arrested.

TRAGEDY AT WOUNDED KNEE

82412

After Sitting Bull was killed, U.S. soldiers swept across the reservation. They intended to round up chiefs who might lead an uprising. On December 29, 1890, soldiers fired on a group of 350 Sioux camped at Wounded Knee Creek. More than half of the Indians, including women and children, were killed, along with their leader, Chief Big Foot, shown here. The massacre at Wounded Knee marked the end of the Ghost Dance religion and the Indian wars.

Before dawn on December 15, 1890, Sioux Indians who had been hired to work as policemen on the Standing Rock Reservation burst into Sitting Bull's cabin and dragged him out. Some of Sitting Bull's friends came to help him. A gunfight erupted. In the confusion that followed, a Sioux policeman named Red Tomahawk put a bullet through Sitting Bull's head.

"I want to tell you that if the Great Spirit had chosen anyone to be the chief of this country, it is myself," Sitting Bull once said. "When I was a boy, the Sioux owned the world. The sun rose and set on their land; they sent 10,000 men into battle. Where are the warriors today? Who slew them? Where are our lands? Who owns them?"

CHRONOLOGY

1830 President Andrew Jackson signs the Indian Removal
Act, giving the U.S. government the power to forcibly
move Indians off their lands

183? An Indian boy named Jumping Badger is born in South
Dakota in March. His father is a Hunkpapa Sioux chief

1846 Jumping Badger proves his bravery in an attack on
Crow warriors and receives the name Sitting Bull from
his father

1851 To ensure the safety of wagon trains on the Oregon
Trail, the government promises food, clothing, and
other goods to the Native Americans. The pact becomes
known as the Treaty of Plenty Rations

1854 On August 19, soldiers under the command of
Lieutenant John L. Grattan are killed after attacking a
Brulé Sioux village near Fort Laramie in Wyoming. The
incident becomes known as the Grattan Massacre

1856 On March 1, General William S. Harney announces he
will appoint all Sioux chiefs

1863 During July, Sioux warriors clash with the army at the
battles of Dead Buffalo Lake and Stony Lake in North
Dakota

1865 Sitting Bull is named chief of the Hunkpapa Sioux

1868 On June 20, Sitting Bull refuses to sign a treaty offered
by Father Pierre-Jean De Smet that creates the Great
Sioux Reservation. One tribe accepts its terms

1869 Sitting Bull is named supreme chief of the Sioux Nation
by six of the seven Sioux tribes

1873 Surveyors planning the North Pacific Railroad arrive in the sacred Black Hills of South Dakota. They are protected by the Seventh Cavalry under the leadership of Lieutenant Colonel George Armstrong Custer

1876 A force of Indian warriors numbering between 3,000 and 12,000 is attacked by the Seventh Cavalry at the Little Bighorn River in Montana on June 25. Custer and all 264 soldiers in his command are slaughtered

1877 Sitting Bull leads the Hunkpapas to Canada in May, where they remain in exile

1881 Starving Hunkpapas return to the United States and on July 12 agree to live on the reservation at Standing Rock in North and South Dakota

1885 Sitting Bull joins Buffalo Bill Cody's Wild West Show in June

1890 Sitting Bull is assassinated on December 15, while under arrest outside his cabin at Standing Rock

GLOSSARY

bayonet–a blade fixed to the end of a rifle that is used to stab the enemy.

cavalry–soldiers who fight while mounted on horses.

centennial–a 100th anniversary.

confluence–a spot where two streams or rivers join.

emissary–a messenger who acts as a representative of the person who sent him or her.

formation–an organized, specific shape.

fortitude–physical and mental strength.

homesteader–a person who settles on land provided by the government.

immersed–completely focused on or absorbed in something.

lance–a long spear used while on horseback.

mandate–authority given to representatives or organizations to pursue a goal.

prospector–a person who explores an area looking for mineral deposits, such as gold.

provisions–a stock of food or necessary supplies.

reprisal–a hostile action taken in revenge for damages or losses suffered.

reservation–a piece of public land set aside where Native Americans were forced to live.

retaliate–to fight back or get revenge.

skirmish–a minor battle that is usually part of a larger conflict.

Sun Dance–a religious rite performed by Native American tribes both as a test of manhood and to inspire visions that could help guide the tribe.

surveyor–a person whose job it is to determine the form and extent of an area of land.

tomahawk–a lightweight axe Native Americans used as a weapon.

valor–bravery.

FURTHER READING

Brennan, Kristine. *Crazy Horse.* Philadelphia: Chelsea House Publishers, 2002.

Brown, Dee. *Bury My Heart at Wounded Knee.* New York: Bantam Books, 1972.

Marcovitz, Hal. *George A. Custer.* Philadelphia: Chelsea House Publishers, 2002.

Overfield, Lloyd J. *The Little Big Horn 1876.* Lincoln: University of Nebraska Press, 1971.

Sandoz, Mari. *The Battle of the Little Big Horn.* Lincoln: University of Nebraska Press, 1978.

St. George, Judith. *To See with the Heart: The Life of Sitting Bull.* New York: G.P. Putnam's Sons, 1996.

Shields, Charles J. *Buffalo Bill Cody.* Philadelphia: Chelsea House Publishers, 2002.

Utley, Robert M. *The Lance and the Shield: The Life and Times of Sitting Bull.* New York: Henry Holt and Co., Inc., 1993.

Whittaker, Frederick. *A Complete Life of General George A. Custer.* Lincoln: University of Nebraska Press, 1993.

Battle of the Little Bighorn, 40-47, 49
Battle of the Rosebud, 42
Bear's Rib, 22, 23
Black Hills ("Paha Sapa"), 13, 33, 35,
    36, 38, 39, 50
Black Moon, 28, 33
Bozeman Trail, 29
Buffalo Bill Cody's Wild West Show,
    53-54

Civil War, 23, 37
Conquering Bear, 21
Crazy Horse, 41, 42, 44
Crook, George, 42, 50
Crow Indians, 8, 9
Custer, George A. "Long Hair," 33,
    36, 37, 38, 42, 43, 44, 46, 49, 52

Dead Buffalo Lake, 23
De Smet, Pierre-Jean, 27, 29-31, 36,
    39

Fort Buford, 25
Fort C. F. Smith, 25
Fort Laramie, Wyoming, 19, 21
Fort Phil Kearny, 25
Fort Pierre, 21
Fort Reno, 25
Four Horns (uncle), 7, 21, 28, 31-32

Gall, 28, 44
Ghost Dance religion, 55-56
Grant, Ulysses S., 52
Grattan, John L., 20-21
Great Sioux Reservation, 29-36, 40,
    50, 52, 54

Harney, William S. "Mad Bear," 21,
    39
Her Holy Door (mother), 13
Hunkpapa Sioux, 7, 8, 9, 14, 17, 20,
    22, 23, 55

Jumping Bull (father), 13

Little Bighorn River, 36, 41, 42-43,
    44, 49, 52

Miles, Nelson A. "Bear Coat," 51

Nez Percé tribe, 51
No Neck, 28
Northern Pacific Railroad, 33

Oregon Trail, 19, 20

Powder River, Montana, 8, 41
Pretty White Cow, 44, 45

Reno, Marcus, 44
Reynolds, Joseph J., 41

Seventh Cavalry ("Long Knives"), 21,
    23, 40, 42, 44, 51, 52
Sitting Bull
    and Battle of the Little Bighorn, 6,
        41, 42, 43, 44, 49, 52
    as chief of Hunkpapa Sioux, 23,
        31-33, 39, 46-47, 51, 56-57
    death of, 55-57
    early years, 9, 13-17
    naming of, 7, 8, 11
Smith, Edward P., 40
Standing Rock, 54
Stony Lake, 23

Tatanka, 16
Treaty of Plenty Rations, 20, 38, 50

Wakan Tanka, 16
White Gut, 28
Wood Mountains, 51
Wovoka, 55

PICTURE CREDITS

HAL MARCOVITZ is a journalist for the *Allentown Morning Call* in Pennsylvania. His other titles for Chelsea House include biographies of the explorers Marco Polo and Francisco Coronado, the Indian guide Sacagawea, and the Apollo astronauts. He lives in Chalfont, Pennsylvania, with his wife, Gail, and daughters, Ashley and Michelle.